KEY IDEAS

The A–Z of Display

Georgina Stein

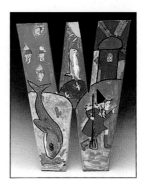

Acknowledgements

First published in 1996 by Folens Limited,
Dunstable and Dublin
Folens Limited
Albert House
Apex Business Centre
Boscombe Road
Dunstable LU5 4RL
England

The author and publisher thank the following:
Peter Codling, Raynes Park High School, London Borough of Merton
Mrs Elizabeth Collison, Rainhill, Prescot, Merseyside
Rev Elizabeth Collison, Rainhill, Prescot, Merseyside
Angela Cook, staff and pupils of Broomwood Hall
Raywen Ford, Co-ordinator, Art Education, Roehampton Institute London
Pamela Pierce, Consultant, Earley, Reading
Phil Poole, Canterbury Christ Church College, Kent
Susan Waterman, Art Education Technician, Roehampton Institute London
Technology Teaching Systems, Monk Road, Alfreton. Tel: 01773 830225 Fax: O1773 830325
BA (QTS) Students, Roehampton Institute London

Also staff and pupils of:
Beechwood Primary School, Berkshire County Council
The Bulmershe School, Berkshire County Council
Colleton Primary School, Berkshire County Council
The Hill Primary School, Berkshire County Council
Kerr Mackie Primary School, Leeds
Radstock County Primary School, Berkshire County Council
St Ann's Church of England Primary School, Rainhill, Merseyside
St Lawrence's Church of England School, Skellingthorpe, Lincoln Education Authority
Waingels Copse School, Berkshire County Council
Willow Bank County Infant School, Berkshire County Council
Willow Bank County Junior School, Berkshire County Council
Woodley Nursery School, Berkshire County Council

Georgina Stein hereby asserts her moral right to be identified as the author of this work in accordance with the Copyright, Designs and Patents Act 1988.
© 1996 Folens Limited, on behalf of the author.
Reprinted 1999
Editor Sarah Peutrill
Layout artist Patricia Hollingsworth

Photographs:
Pauline Bottrill, Bethesda, Maryland, USA: top 17, top 37.
Colleton Primary School: bottom 8, top 53.
Phil Everitt, Canterbury Christ Church College, Kent: bottom 19, top 22.
Sandra Hall, Radstock County Primary School: top 35, top 40.
Carolyn Liburn, Kerr Mackie Primary School: bottom 17, bottom 29, top 34, bottom 37.
St Lawrence's Church of England School: bottom 13, bottom 34.
Georgina Stein, Senior Lecturer in Education, Roehampton Institute: 4, 6, 7, 9, 10, 11, 12, top 13, 14, 15, top 19, bottom 20, bottom 22, 25, 28, top 29, 32, 33, bottom 35, 38, bottom 39, bottom 40, bottom 43, 44, 45, top 47, 48, 49, 50, 51, top 52, 56, 57 and all photographs of letters.
Andrea Stephens, Radstock County Primary School: top 8, bottom 23, top 31, top 39.
Woodley Nursery School: bottom 53.
Willow Bank County Infant School: bottom 52.
Ray Young and Georgina Stein: 5, 16, top 20, 21, top 23, 24, 26, 27, 30, bottom 31, 36, 41, 42, top 43, 46, bottom 47, 54, 55.
Illustrations Paul C Allen
Cover image Georgina Stein
Cover photograph Pete Ryan
Series design Andy Bailey
Cover design Kim Ashby and DFM

British Library Cataloguing in Publication Data. A catalogue record for this book is available from the British Library.

Printed in Hong Kong through World Print

ISBN 1 85276914-9

Contents

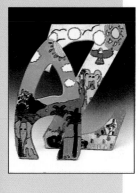

Displays are the windows of the curriculum – a celebration of teaching and learning. Imagine a classroom with bare walls and closed storage units or a school without decorated entrances and attractive assembly halls.

Creating a visually-stimulating environment in our schools can give children a greater interest in the world around them as well as in the subjects they are studying. A colourful display on the life cycle of frogs can develop an interest in science. A display on Lowry might encourage a budding artist.

This book suggests imaginative ideas for creating displays in classrooms, assembly halls and school entrances. It outlines methods for designing, with confidence and competence, stimulating display areas, even with limited space and resources.

Some schools may only have small dark areas, such as above a sink, to use for display. Ideas for brightening up such areas are given in D – Decorating problem areas. Alternatively, other schools may have huge spaces that need to be covered. Several ideas for this are given in section E – Eye-catchers.

The displays suggested throughout the book use readily-available resources, from cardboard boxes to sweet wrappers and labels. Cardboard boxes can be used as the support for three-dimensional displays, such as the Autumn collection shown on page 5, or to make wall-mounted displays, such as those on page 7. Colourful wrappers and labels can be used to create a shop or a publicity montage.

This sun-screen decoration was made from coloured card. Details on how to make it can be found on page 51, which also shows how the idea was developed and the screen made more attractive.

4

In addition, the book offers a variety of tips for techniques. There are hints on balancing mobiles, joining and hanging techniques and tips for reusing existing displays.

The sample templates on pages 58 to 64 can be enlarged on a photocopier and used to create the displays indicated.

It is not intended that these ideas are for the teacher alone. Many of the displays can be created by the children. In doing so they will gain knowledge and skills in the art of display, in a range of techniques and in handling a variety of materials.

This fabric snowman was glued to the background of this wall-hanger. Further ideas for hangers can be found on pages 20 and 21.

Displays should provoke a response from the children. This tactile display was used to stimulate language and was regularly changed and rearranged by the children.

Introduction

5

Three-dimensional wall-mounted displays

Some wall-mounted displays are arranged flat against the surface of the display board. There are many simple ways, however, to create a more eye-catching, three-dimensional effect, such as by attaching objects to the wall or by using special attachment techniques.

These three-dimensional paper flowers were stapled to the display board. A close-up is shown on the right.

Attachments

1 **Summer blooms**

- The tree was created from paper which was partly wrapped around real twigs and branches. These were decorated with tissue-paper flowers, which were stapled to the display. Florist wire was used to create the flower stems.

6

A small cardboard box was used to make
the washing machine in this display.

2 Frogs' holiday

■ The washing machine was stapled to the wall and a small frog
glued to its base. The characters in the scene were created from
card and tissue-paper. The washing line held items made from
fabric and paper and was only attached at the top, giving a three-
dimensional effect.

The house in the ark was created
from a cardboard box which was
stapled to the wall.

3 Noah's Ark

■ The house within the ark
was created from a box.
This was covered with
cardboard strips to make
up the boat. These strips
were joined together and
wrapped around the
house. Some of the
animals were attached to
circles of card, to make
them stand out and then
stapled to the wall.

Display tip

■ Cardboard containers of various sizes and
shapes are very useful when attempting to
create three-dimensional effects. Generally,
cardboard boxes can be opened up, then
stapled to the wall and reassembled before the
item to be displayed is taped to the container.

KEY IDEAS – *The A–Z of Display*

Bored with borders?

Borders define a display. Traditionally, they have been used to create a regular perimeter around a display with an equal margin surrounding the edge, forming a boundary. The following borders were designed to reflect and enhance the displays they surround. They were created from fabric, card, paper, paint and other resources, using a variety of different techniques.

> Paintings displayed to their best by using complementary fabric and tissue-paper flowers.

1 | Fabric and flowers

■ This display of children's impressions of Van Gogh's *Cornfield and Cypresses* shows how the use of subject matter in the paintings can be repeated in the arrangement of the display. The floral hanging fabric was carefully selected to complement the scenes and the tissue paper poppies are three-dimensional representations of the flowers in the paintings. They were attached to the board with drawing pins.

2 | Using leaves

■ The artificial leaves complement the corn dollies and create a three-dimensional feel. They were spaced out along a length of string and attached to the wooden surround with clear tape. Alternatively, leaf borders can be made from paper or fabric, using the templates on page 58.

> Artificial leaves used here to enhance the natural resources in the display.

8

Using classroom curtains as an effective display device.

3 Classroom curtains and drapes

■ The curtains in this display are a permanent feature of this classroom that were used to create a border. Fabric to complement the curtains was stapled to the wall on the opposite side to define the edge of the display area.

Other ideas

The content of a display can determine the border type, for example:
■ spring – daffodil heads made from cardboard egg cartons and card
■ science – skeleton bones cut from white card with black felt-tipped pen edges
■ stories – letters cut from large stencils.
Try using:
■ fabric – plaiting strips together to create a textured border
■ illustrations from magazines and comics.

9

Contrasting and combining colour

The colour used in a display is very important. The natural light available in a classroom or school generally influences where a particular display should be mounted or arranged. Dark corners can be brought to life with the right choice of colours, but this only works if the content of the display and the choice of colours are appropriately matched. Techniques using colour can create interesting effects and will enhance a display area. Marbling and mosaic work helps the children to give texture to a large image area quickly and effectively.

The complementary colours used in this split display allow the two areas to be viewed separately and together.

1 A split display

- The seascape is a continuous sheet of blue paper. The seabed is made from individual sheets of A4 paper mounted together, supported by green strips that allow the paper to be slipped in. To create a new effect the green can be easily exchanged for a different colour.

Marbled coloured paper is an attractive alternative to plain sugar-paper.

2 Transforming sugar- paper

- Large red, pink and purple sugar-paper shapes were cut to represent the inside of the cave and their appearance transformed by splattering them with blue and white paint. The shapes were arranged randomly on the wall, with a space left between the wall and the paper to give a three-dimensional effect. The characters in the display were made from painted sugar-paper and were stapled to the wall-board.

A variety of materials, tools and resources were used to create this 'blue' colour corner.

3 | Brightening a dull corner

- This display demonstrates how printing and collage can be brought together to form a colour corner. The random patterns were introduced by mounting them on blue paper. A variety of coloured materials were glued on to card to show textures within the corner. The use of a single colour brings together all the elements of the display effectively.
- A colour corner can be a feature of any classroom or area within a school and can be used in many ways: from introducing a particular colour to young children, through to helping older children gain knowledge and understanding of tones, tints and colour matching.

4 | Using colour to create texture

A mosaic creates a colourful and interesting pattern.

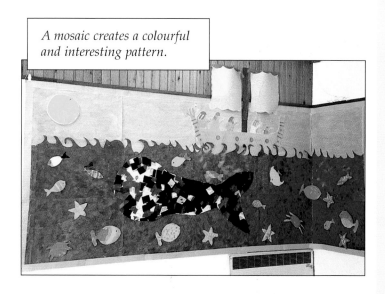

- The surface of the whale was covered with wallpaper paste and coloured tissue shapes were tipped on. The sea was created by marbling large sheets of sugar-paper. Fish and other shapes were made to stand out by painting them in distinct colours. Templates that can be used to create the fish can be found on page 58.

Other ideas

- Decorate a wooden clothing peg with felt-tipped pens and coloured paper.
- Drip food colouring with an eye dropper on to different types of paper, such as blotting paper, paper towels and rice paper. Hang them on a washing line to dry.

11

Decorating problem areas

Sometimes display areas can present problems; walls and ceilings can be particularly difficult to attach to and large areas can be difficult to cover quickly. A variety of techniques can be used with paper to create colourful decorations for free-standing, wall-mounted and ceiling-hanging displays.

1 Lavender bags

■ This free-standing display was created to brighten the corner of the corridor. The log is a permanent fixture and can be used time and time again. The lavender bags were fixed to the log with drawing pins. A decorative bowl of paper hyacinths was attached to the wall with Blu-Tack ®. Tissue and sugar-paper flowers were pinned behind it.

A decorative free-standing corner display.

This display was created to brighten the plain wall by using a free-standing vase and sunflowers attached to the wall.

2 Sunflowers and vase

■ Vases of flowers and wall-mounted flowers were displayed from one end of a long corridor to the other. The petals were cut from card and glued to the back of a circle of card, then attached to the wall with masking tape.

Decorations

12

Decorations

3 | Handy flowers

■ Each flower was made from four paper hand prints that were attached to the back of card circles decorated with tissue-paper. They were used to create a bed of flowers in a springtime display.

4 | Classroom sink

■ Matching drapes and cardboard suns were used here to brighten the sink area. The orange drapes were carefully selected for their colours and arranged to enhance the plain white board.

■ The drapes were supported on a garden cane that was attached at the corners of the classroom. Fabric suns were suspended from the ceiling and the orange drape. The summer sun poems were circles of white card with sun rays made from strips of yellow and red card.

An awkward corner cheered up by bright summer suns.

Eye-catchers

Large wall-mounted displays

Large wall-mounted display areas can be designed to demonstrate a variety of techniques and materials that can be used generally in the classroom. Areas can be covered quickly when the children work together.

These very large eye-catchers, when displayed in an entrance or assembly hall, attract the attention of the children and demonstrate ways in which they can produce their own work.

A large wall area was quickly transformed with large leaves and stems. The complete display is shown below.

1 Paper printing, pattern making and folding

■ These leaf shapes were decorated with pencil and printed with paint. The display board was rapidly transformed when the sugar-paper stems and leaves were attached using staples. Leaves to photocopy and enlarge are on page 58.

14

Large sheets of paper were decorated by individual children before they were collectively wall-mounted.

2 Repeated patterns

- The children were given large sheets of sugar-paper. They divided the sheets into 12 equal parts and created their own repeating patterns with paint.

3 A quilt

- A double quilt cover was decorated by a number of children of different ages from around the school, each doing a square. Appropriate materials were chosen to represent each animal. Fabric glue was used to secure the images in place after they were completed.

A wall-mounted double quilt, decorated by the children.

15

Frames

Attractive display frames

Different resource materials such as wood, fabric, card and paper can be used to frame pictures and illustrations for display in a classroom gallery or elsewhere in the school. When children's work is framed, it can be easily transported and displays can be quickly changed or rearranged.

1 Mounting a fabric picture

- This fabric picture was mounted on card. Ribbons were glued around the edge of the card to create a frame and a decorative bow and ribbon hangers were stapled to the edge.

Ribbons can be used to good effect when displaying paintings or collages.

2 A wooden frame

- This three-dimensional house was mounted on coloured corrugated plastic. A variety of materials including card, feathers and fabric were cut and glued in place. The joints of the frame were cut using a mitre-block and a tenon saw and glued on to the corrugated plastic. Weights were used to hold the frame secure as the glue dried. (If a mitre-block is not available, 90 degree butt-joints can be used for this frame.)

A wooden frame, matching the style of the picture.

16

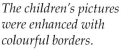
The children's pictures were enhanced with colourful borders.

3 | Coloured frames

- This frame effect was created by leaving a space around the pictures to be decorated using felt-tip pens. The pictures were then stapled to the wall.

4 | Cardboard frames

- These cardboard frames are ideal for displaying the tissue-paper patterns. The two rims were glued together after the shapes were completed. They were mounted on to a window to allow the light to shine through the display.

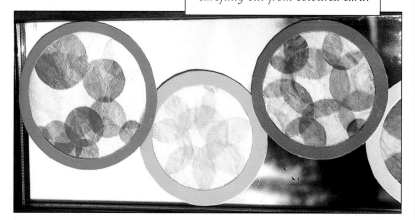
These circular frames were carefully cut from coloured card.

Other ideas

- Frames can be used time and time again by attaching strips of layered cardboard behind a cardboard frame to create a slot in which pictures and illustrations can be placed. Some ideas for creative frames for the children to decorate can be found on page 59.
- Glass clip frames are useful for creating displays of special pictures or illustrations in areas that the children frequently visit, such as entrance halls.

17

Displaying work throughout the school

A gallery space for viewing children's work and that of famous artists in an entrance hall, library or some other communal area will encourage the children to think carefully about the audience of their work. It also gives children and teachers the opportunity to share their ideas, knowledge and understanding of different materials and techniques.

A gallery exhibition space can be created in any classroom and the children can take responsibility for collecting the contributions from other children in different year groups. Exhibiting work to show progression in the use of specific materials can also help to inform parents about how children develop skills, knowledge and understanding from year to year. The work should be arranged so that it can be viewed or studied easily.

Galleries

A gallery in the school entrance, displayed at a height that can be easily viewed.

1 An entrance hall gallery

■ In this gallery with the theme of 'buildings', adequate space was left between the illustrations in order that each item can be clearly observed. The children's individual portfolios are pinned to the wall in a way that makes them accessible to the other children.

This gallery was designed for a special event with large display screens used in and around the assembly hall.

2 Using screens

■ The brightly-coloured illustrations were pinned to the neutral hessian boards to display them at their best. Alternatively, pictures could be attached to a large upright box.

18

3 A picture gallery in the classroom

- Picture galleries in individual classrooms can be used to encourage children from other classes to visit and view work. An open event could be planned to enable the children to see what goes on in other classrooms.

The yellow display board is framed with blue and echoes the double-mounted illustrations.

The fabric in this gallery is a permanent display feature.

4 A corner gallery

- This 'corner gallery' was enhanced by attaching clay suns with safety pins to the fabric drapes that border the edge of the display.

KEY IDEAS – *The A–Z of Display*

19

Creating attractive hanging displays

Ceiling and wall spaces provide valuable display areas in the classroom. Washing lines can make effective use of space and fabric drapes can be adapted to accommodate hangers.

Hooks, pegs and fasteners can be used for temporary attachment in these display areas, ensuring that they can be changed regularly or rearranged without difficulty.

Hangers

1 A fabric wall-hanger

- This large fabric hanging display was made with felt leaf shapes (templates on page 58) sewn on to a fabric backdrop with a sewing machine (fabric glue can be used with younger children). A cord was used to suspend the hanger from the wall.

- Small hangers can be created by individual children. Dowels can be used instead of rods and wool can be plaited to create a suspension cord.

2 Hanging paper houses

- These paper houses were made from card which was cut and folded into two parts. They were straddled across a washing line pulley which was suspended from the ceiling.

Wooden rods at the top and bottom of this wall-hanger hold the fabric securely in place.

These hanging houses were decorated on both sides.

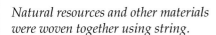
3 A woven natural resource hanger

■ This large wall-mounted hanger was suspended from a branch attached to brackets that were secured to the wall. It was created by a group of children working separately on weaving together natural resources with other items, including construction straws and strips of fabric. When individual sections were complete, they were strung together. Leaves threaded through the string disguised the joints.

Natural resources and other materials were woven together using string.

Other ideas

Old-fashioned rack-type pulley systems are ideal for creating hanging space in the classroom. They are suitable for:
■ jokes one side with the responses on the other
■ questions one side and answers on the other
■ descriptions one side – 'It is big and barks!' – and illustrations on the other
■ fun sums one side and answers on the other, eg 6 x 2 equals ... .

21

Starting points for creating displays

Themes and topics are generally the focus of displays in schools. However, good display ideas can spring from just about anywhere. They can be generated by introducing a resource, a concept or a problem to the children and by asking them to use either the resource in a display of their choice or to create a display to solve the problem.

There are endless possibilities for the focus of displays. The following examples demonstrate the idea of an 'inspiring display'.

A variety of different types of clowns were created for this display.

1 A theme-based approach to display

- The children were introduced to the theme of clowns and they brought in 'clown-like' characters from home. Different types of clown characters were made by the children and they were arranged over an extensive area which included wall-mounted, hanging and free-standing clowns.

This 'corner shop' was designed by older children for younger children.

2 Problem solving

- A shop as a resource was needed by the younger children in the school. The older children were presented with the problem and made suggestions to the teacher as to how the younger children could make their own shop.
- The backdrop to the shop was created by decorating large sheets of sugar-paper with pictures of cans. Images of food were cut from magazines and mounted on to paper before being covered with protective plastic sheeting. The children brought in the items for sale. Small buckets were introduced as shopping baskets.

22

This simple arrangement has been created inside a large cooker box.

3 Teddy bears

- This corner display was made from a very large cardboard box. The window was a sheet of white paper and the curtains were stapled in place. Boxes were covered with brown paper to create the television. The image on the television was computer generated, as was the clock on the wall.

- Small items such as the table, ornaments and the mat were introduced into the display. The large teddy was dressed up in leggings stuffed with newspaper, a child's T-shirt and a cardigan. Socks conceal the string that was tied tightly to hold the newspaper in place.

An awkward wall is livened up with Humpty Dumpty replicas.

4 A papier mâché solution for a walled area

- When presented with the problem of covering a wall top with a display, naturally the children thought of Humpty Dumpty. These were made from balloons covered with painted papier mâché. The legs were made from folded strips of coloured paper that were attached to the heads with PVA glue.

23

Ways of joining materials

Using the right joining materials for specific tasks is vitally important when creating any display. Knowing how different materials respond when specific types of adhesives are used can make all the difference to how a display looks; good work can be ruined if the wrong joining materials or techniques are used. Experimenting with materials to see 'what works best' is a necessary part of development for the children. Allow them to think for themselves.

Simple activities can be designed to help them experiment with a variety of materials, tools and equipment, giving them valuable knowledge and understanding of the properties of different materials.

1 A view from the window

- A selection of materials were given to the children and they were asked to use some of them to create a display. They used various types of glue, staples, ribbons and Velcro® fastener.
- Everyday items can be used to try out different joining and attachment techniques, presenting the children with a challenge.

A free-standing display made from reclaimed materials.

An environmental display showing how different materials can be used creatively.

2 No fishing

- This circular display was divided into three sections and different materials were attached to the board.
- The children were asked to experiment with different types of adhesive (PVA, wallpaper paste, glue and masking tape), sticking materials such as: pasta shapes, dried beans, felt, cotton, wet and dried leaves, chalk, charcoal, paint, felt-tipped pens and cork.

KEY IDEAS – *The A–Z of Display* © Folens (not copiable)

3 Paper weaving

■ The balloon was made from card covered in tissue-paper. The woven paper basket was attached to the balloon with strips of card. Staples were used to secure the basket and the balloon to the display board. The woven paper was securely joined so that it would hold the fabric doll passengers.

4 Grandparents

■ These 'grandparents' were stuffed with newspaper to make them three-dimensional. String, paper clips, staples and different types of glue held them firmly in place.

Paper was woven together to form the basket of this hot-air balloon.

This wall-mounted display was made using a variety of joining techniques.

Other ideas

Create a 'joining' display board: give the children a variety of materials and ask them to create a display that will demonstrate how things can be joined. They will require:
■ string and wool
■ dressmaking pins
■ safety pins
■ laces
■ zips
■ wire
■ strips of wood.

25

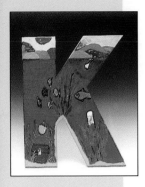

Knick-knacks

Making cheap but effective displays

'Knick-knacks' describes small items that can be made cheaply. These can be created by the children from reclaimed materials, such as card and paper. Asking them to make specific things for particular display purposes can be stimulating and challenging. Display items could be commissioned, particularly if they are to be placed in special areas, such as the school entrance. Retaining work made by the children also demonstrates that their work is valued by the school.

1 Paper vases and flowers

- This display of vases shows how knick-knacks can be arranged simply and attractively. Patterns were drawn on to sheets of paper and attached to strong card with masking tape. The vase templates were then cut out using a craft knife or scissors. The sections were taped together with masking tape and painted over with a mixture of PVA and paint. A sample template can be found on page 60.

Colourful cardboard vases, containing artificial flowers, that were commissioned by the headteacher.

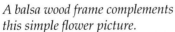

A balsa wood frame complements this simple flower picture.

2 A framed picture

- This felt and thread flower design was made from a square of corrugated plastic sheet surrounded by balsa wood. A plaited woollen hanger was attached to the rear of the picture with masking tape. A simple woollen bee with net wings was glued to the corner of the frame. Framed pictures such as this are easy to make and can be transported easily.

26

3 | Tissue-paper flowers

■ These flowers were made using ordinary large tissues. First the mid-points were marked with a pencil. Squeezing between the thumb and index finger, a pattern was gently stroked on to the tissues using different coloured felt-tipped pens. They were then attached to large paper construction straws with masking tape. Green crêpe or tissue-paper was finally wrapped around the straw stems using clear tape.

The jug of flowers shows how the work of different children can be brought together in a simple display.

Other ideas

■ Challenge the children to create knick-knacks of their own design. Give each child the same materials and access to the same equipment.
■ They could make their knick-knacks to complement a particular display theme such as 'animals', 'in the park' or 'by the sea'.

Knick-knacks

27

Labelling displays

The lettering on a display, and how it is arranged, plays an important role in linking the content of the display with the audience. Investing time in 'getting it right' can make all the difference to the overall effect of a display.

1 Shadow lettering

- This shadow lettering was created using different coloured letter stencils. The yellow links with the content of the display and to the plain border.

- When using letters in a display it is advisable to ensure that they are attached to each other before they are attached to the wall. If the letters are to be used over and over again, the attachments should be made with either masking tape or some other temporary attachment material.

A lettering technique that links with the display.

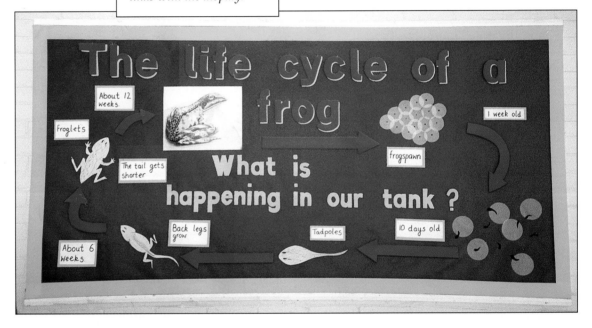

The zigzag shapes attract the children's attention.

2 Animal sounds

- These display labels were attached with masking tape so that they can be used time and time again.

3 Letter bubbles

■ Attracting attention to words can be achieved by surrounding them with vibrant and interesting shapes. White card was used for these thought bubbles that were attached to the wall with masking tape. Each part of the bubble was attached separately.

Making use of an inaccessible area by using eye-catching speech and thought bubbles.

The lettering technique used in this display reflects its content.

4 Using pre-formed letters

■ This display uses a combination of letter stencils from magazines and newspapers that have been glued on to the card background.

Other ideas

■ 'Shaped' lettering, with the letters following curved lines is easy to do and very effective, as shown:

The Three Bears   The Three Bears   The Three Bears

■ Create a 'letter bank' to be used time and time again by teachers and children. This involves using letter stencils of various sizes on a variety of materials including: card and paper, corrugated card, felt, and fine and coarse sandpaper. Some materials may require covering with plastic coating for protection, but others such as the sandpaper will not.

■ Make letters wobbly by using double-sided tape to attach one end of a strip of clear plastic to a letter and the other end to the wall.

29

Creating and displaying mobiles

Displaying mobiles in the classroom can present problems as they can be difficult to hang when they are not properly balanced. There are different ways in which mobiles can be arranged so that they can be successfully displayed.

Balancing the characters on a mobile can be achieved by using pre-formed shape templates. This removes 'guessing' to see if the mobile will or will not balance after the shapes have been formed by the children. The templates can be used as a 'mock-up' for the mobile. By creating a trapeze or ladder-style mobile – rather than the crossed bar type – it is possible for mobiles, made from light-weight materials such as card, paper, papier mâché and balsa wood to be displayed effectively.

Fish hung from a bar to create an effective display device.

A balsa wood mobile, balanced by trial and error.

1 Creating a trapeze

■ The fish were made from papier mâché covered balloons, coated with layers of crêpe paper. They were attached to the wooden trapeze bar by string threaded through crêpe paper. The bar was suspended from the ceiling by string attached to two ceiling hooks. The trapeze can be used time and time again for displaying different types of mobiles.

2 Wild animals

■ A number of children worked together to create this mobile . Small hooks were inserted into the balsa wood to enable the thread to be attached. Felt-tipped pens were used for the decoration. Templates for some of the animals can be found on page 61.

3 The house on the rock stood firm

■ This mobile was part of a wall-mounted display. Shiny cardboard raindrops were attached to the stiff card clouds. Thread was used to attach the clouds to a self-adhesive ceiling hook.

4 Flying pigs

■ This pigs mobile was made from balsa wood. The pigs on the front of the rectangular strip of wood were glued in place; they were arranged to make the mobile balance.

Integrating a wall-mounted display with a mobile.

A balsa wood mobile, cleverly balanced by the matching pigs on the crossbar.

Other ideas

■ Box mobiles can be an attractive alternative to wall or ceiling-hanging mobiles. The advantage of creating a mobile in a box is that it allows children to interact with the display. Sophisticated box mobiles can be powered by a simple switched motor.

31

Creating and using different types of notice-boards

Notice-boards can be changed to display up-to-date information on a regular basis; even young children can be encouraged to 'look to see' what's different. Information displayed on notice-boards can be frequently used and continually changed, so the display should be placed in an appropriate and accessible area. They should be designed to remain attractive regardless of the changes that take place.

A news room notice-board showing articles of interest cut from newspapers.

1 News room bulletin board

■ Any article of interest to the children can be displayed on the news room bulletin board including: newspaper articles, cartoons, jokes and competitions. Rather than just pinning the articles to the wall, the children should be encouraged to display their notices carefully. A theme or focus for the week could be chosen and groups could take responsibility for collecting and displaying the information.

2 Our birthday train

■ The birthday train is a good example of a permanent display that can be viewed by the children, but is inaccessible as they do not have to make any changes to the information shown on the display.

KEY IDEAS – *The A–Z of Display*

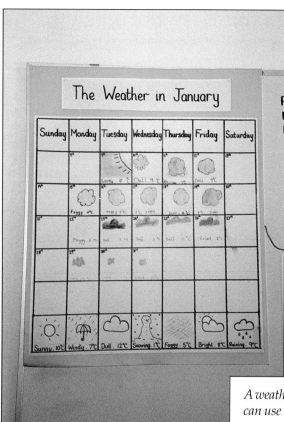

3 Recording information

■ This display board was laminated so that it can be used time and time again. Each day the children can add to it by drawing a picture on a separate piece of paper and sticking it on with masking tape. Alternatively, permanent laminated pictures could be made and simply picked out by the children each day. The codes for the weather are shown at the bottom of the chart.

A weather chart that the children can use to record information.

4 An events display board

■ Quick changes can be easily made to the content of this display as the names are attached with drawing pins. The pictures and the months are permanent.

A quick and colourful events display board.

Materials and techniques for close observation

By paying close attention to detail, children gain valuable knowledge and understanding of the subjects they are studying. They should be given the opportunity to: observe detail in a variety of situations and contexts that relate to subjects within the curriculum, identify various distinguishing characteristics, record their perceptions in a number of different ways using materials and techniques they have selected and display their observations to enhance the details they have observed.

A display of children's observations of night-time creatures.

1 Nocturnal creatures

■ This display demonstrates how a small group of children studying life processes and living things recorded what they had discovered about two night-time creatures.

The children chose the blue background and the black sugar-paper and chalk materials to record their observations of owls and bats. The creatures were glued in place and tiny shiny shapes were added to represent stars.

Recording similarities and differences within the group.

2 Who's who?

■ This display technique of using silhouettes (see display tip) attached to a white painted background, was chosen by the children to record the similarities and differences between the group. They have also recorded their observations in writing.

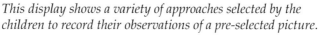

This display shows a variety of approaches selected by the children to record their observations of a pre-selected picture.

3 | Our favourite pictures

■ Pastels, chalk, pencil crayons, watercolours and paint were used to represent the floral displays. White surrounds were used for mounting the artists' pictures and the children's work was mounted on black. The vase of flowers placed in front of the wall-mounted display reflected its content.

A display using pastels, crayons and paints to record observations.

4 | Big cats

■ After researching 'big cats' the children were asked to use one of three types of media to define a detailed image of a cat of their choice. They could choose which paper they would use, but many selected black or white sugar-paper.

Display tip

To create the 'head and shoulders' silhouettes:
■ sit the subject close to a paper screen, side facing the paper to get a profile view
■ use a light source such as an overhead projector to illuminate the subject
■ use a pencil to outline the image that is projected on to the screen
■ cut out the template of the image and transfer it on to black sugar-paper.

35

Using paper to create interesting effects

Different cutting, shaping and joining techniques can radically transform the appearance of paper. By trying out different techniques, children will gain valuable knowledge and understanding of its properties. Paper products such as bags and plates can also be used creatively to produce interesting displays.

1 Paper twirls

- Each of the paper twirls on the wall-mounted display was created from different sheets of card, decorated with elaborate designs. Felt-tipped pens were used to create the intricate patterns. The twirls were cut and twisted into place, glued on to white card and stapled to the wall, leaving them standing proud of the wall to create a three-dimensional effect.

These paper twirls create a colourful and interesting display.

2 Paper faces

- White card was cut into an oval shape and sections were removed to create the expressions on the faces. They were then mounted on a black background. Sample templates can be found on page 63.
- Experimenting with card can be expensive so newspapers and magazines can be used to try out different techniques.

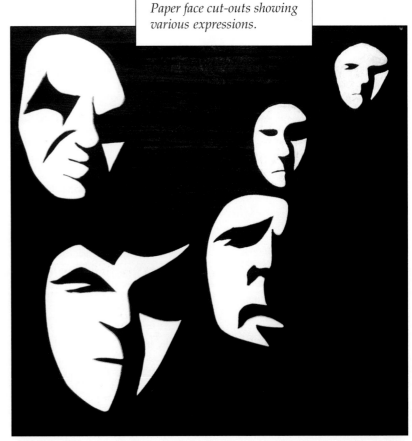

Paper face cut-outs showing various expressions.

36

An impressive paper plate dragon, suspended from the ceiling.

3 The dragon mobile

- A length of string was threaded through patterned paper plates and crêpe paper.
- The dragon was displayed hanging from the ceiling and was attached at three points with nylon threaded through ceiling hooks.

4 Paper bag puppets

- The bags were decorated with a variety of materials and stapled to the wall-board. They can be detached and replaced easily.

Do you like our paper bag puppets?

Other ideas

- Paper plates are inexpensive and they can be used in many different ways. Here are a few ways in which children can use them:
  - decorative celebration plates
  - wall-mounted faces, with woollen hair and features
  - fast-food publicity – using a variety of materials.
- Paper techniques include: folding, curling, weaving, plaiting, feathering, concertinas, rolling, twisting and papier mâché.

37

Modifying permanent displays

Impressive interactive wall-mounted displays can be used in any classroom and designed so that they can be used over and over again. Permanent displays with parts that can be detached and changed remain useful for a long time and will continue to impress.

1 A birthday calendar

- These decorated elephants are made from sugar-paper and stapled firmly to a wall-board. The pencil sketch faces represent the month in which a particular child was born. The month labels attached to the display board are permanent, but the faces and the question labels are attached with masking tape and can be easily removed.

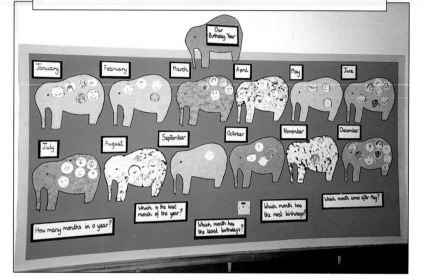

This elephant calendar can be easily altered for new children.

- This display can be changed and replaced with illustrations to represent special calendar events such as religious festivals, the number of days in each month and typical seasonal weather, such as clouds, sun, snow and rain.

The articles on the washing line can be easily replaced to create a new effect.

2 Hanging out the washing

- The idea for this display came from a story that featured washing clothes. The washing on the line can be changed regularly. The line is wrapped around the tree and attached to the cardboard post in the picture.

38

3 The big red bus

- The characters in the bus are the children. They were made from different types of paper and fabric that were glued in pairs on to the square white window shapes. The windows were temporarily attached to the bus with masking tape, allowing them to be moved to a different place on the bus.

- The display was positioned in an accessible place to allow the children to rearrange the passengers to different positions within the bus.
- The windows display can be detached and other windows can be inserted to show different colours and shapes.

The windows on the bus can be removed and their positions changed.

The numbers in this display remain the same, but the images can be regularly changed.

4 A number board

- The permanent background of this wall-mounted display was made from colourful sugar-paper. The illustrations are attached with masking tape so that they can be detached. The children used shape templates to create the images within each rectangle and the numbers were made from stencils. Some

sample templates are on page 62.
- Themes can be used for the pictures such as different fruits, animals and flowers.

KEY IDEAS – *The A–Z of Display*

Creating displays that emulate an original source

To reproduce an image or figure that is in the style of, or emulates, an original source can be challenging for the children, particularly if they are required to create a likeness from memory and not from close observation. The use of a variety of drawing, painting and modelling techniques should be encouraged throughout the process of creating two-dimensional and three-dimensional representations. Subjects across the curriculum can be used as 'starting points' for reproductions.

Reproductions

A display using art as a starting point with the work of a famous artist.

William Morris (1834-1896) designed wallpaper for Royal homes in Victorian times.

1 | William Morris wallpaper

■ The material drape and vase of dried flowers were shown to the children for a short time. They were then removed to encourage them to have their own creative impact. The painted designs created by the children were wall-mounted alongside the drape and the flowers.

2 | Impressions of Lowry

■ This display was created using five painted sugar-paper panels. The mills and houses were illustrated separately and arranged on the painted panels by the children, ensuring that the joining areas remained clear. Where appropriate, a building was used to straddle the joints. The size and height of the 'match-stick figures' were agreed before they were illustrated.

Lowry's famous style is reproduced by the children.

Impressions of Lowry

These displays show how everyday items can be used as a starting point.

3 | Hats and irons

■ These models of hats and irons were made from painted corrugated cardboard, layered and glued together to create three-dimensional displays. The hats were supported by stands of tins and bottles that were covered in papier mâché. These can be painted and used for many different display purposes. The irons are standing on a selection of painted boxes.

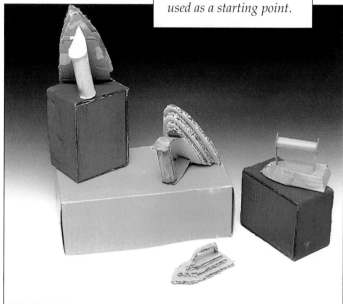

Other ideas

Everyday items can be the subject of three-dimensional reproductions and they can be made from a variety of different materials. For example:
■ flowers – tissue and crêpe paper
■ bowls and containers – papier mâché
■ fans – folded paper
■ boats – balsa wood with paper sails
■ houses – cardboard boxes
■ people – clay and plasticine.

41

Creating display stands

The ability to refresh a display area quickly, or to change a specific area regularly, needs suitable display resources. Simple time-saving cardboard display stands and frames can be made by teachers and older children. They are very useful classroom items. If a number of designs are made they can be combined in a variety of ways. Younger children will be able to create imaginative designs by decorating the cardboard with different materials.

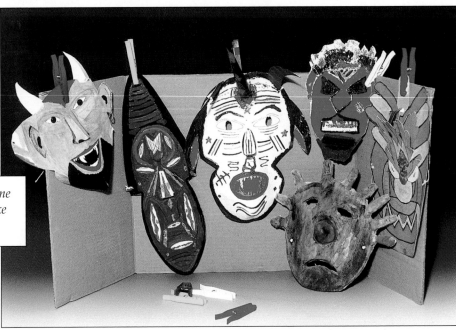

A theatre design frame that is simple to make and decorate.

1 Cardboard theatre

■ This theatre was cut from a cardboard box with the folds in the box creating the wings of the theatre. The masks were made from card and paper and were attached to the frame by washing line pegs. The frame was not decorated so that the masks could be seen clearly against the neutral background.

2 Corner shelves

■ The shelves on this stand were fitted into slits that were cut into the backdrop. It will fit neatly into any corner and is easy to change, store and transport. A number of these stalls, when used together, enable sections of a display to be viewed at different angles.

Using a cardboard stand to display natural objects.

42

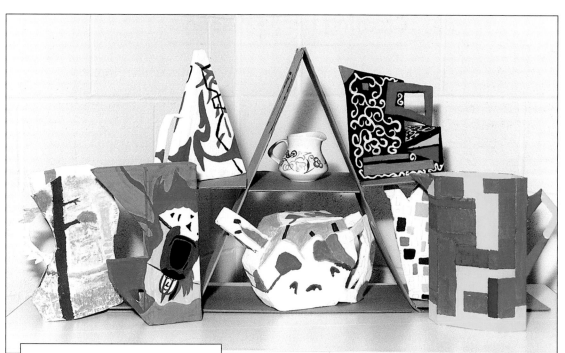

Stand displaying cardboard jugs.

3 Triangular stacker

- This stand was made by cutting slots into individual strips of cardboard. It enables the items on display to be viewed at different levels.

4 Creating different levels

- A variety of boxes were used to raise the level of this display, which has been draped with green fabric. This technique allows the children to view the items from a different angle.

This display of woodland objects was created simply and quickly.

43

Textiles

Creating tactile displays

Textiles can be used to create fascinating displays. By cutting, shaping and joining them, children gain valuable knowledge and understanding of their different properties. Knowledge of materials provides insight into the contribution that specific textiles can make to the structure of clothing and household items. All of the ideas are designed to promote tactile displays that include textured images and pictures which combine a variety of techniques.

Numerous decorative techniques were captured on this large triangular hanger. The detail is shown on the left.

1 Fun with fabric

■ Wax crayons, fabric crayons, felt-tipped pens and coloured pencils were used on felt fabric, cotton and hessian. The materials were attached with fabric glue.

2 Fabric collage

■ Shape templates were used to create this fabric collage wall-hanger. The children selected fabrics that they thought represented the areas they were creating and the images were roughly sewn in place. The materials included wadding for the cloud, dish cloth material for the pond, cotton wool for the sheep and wool for the hair.

This collage shows how appropriate materials were selected for each component.

44

The textile tree is a permanent fixture, although the leaves, butterflies, spiders and other small items are only temporarily attached. Some of the detail is shown above.

3 Temporary attachment

■ This large wall-hanging display was created by children from different year groups. Velcro® fastener and press-studs were attached to the fixtures, such as the animals, in order that changes can take place. The display was securely fixed to the wall in an accessible position, so that the children could make regular changes to its appearance.

This display shows how textiles have been incorporated into a wall-mounted display.

4 Creating texture with fabric

■ 'The pig and the turkey' was made from a variety of materials. Card, sticky paper, tissue and crêpe paper were combined with textiles to create a textured surface.

45

Tips for displays in general

This section contains useful tips for creating displays generally. They can be used in any classroom. Display boards such as the hessian-covered notice-board could be made available to the children to encourage them to create their own displays. It is also a good opportunity to allow them to work co-operatively.

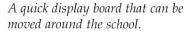

A quick display board that can be moved around the school.

1 Moveable display boards

- This hessian-covered notice-board was inexpensive to buy and allows the children to arrange their work easily. Such boards can be covered and changed quickly and transported to other areas in the school when necessary, such as for a special assembly.
- These funny faces were made from paper. The eyes were computer generated on to A4 sheets of white paper – but they could be easily reproduced using circles of card and felt-tipped pens. The children were asked to transform them into characters of their choice. The finished faces were attached to circles of card that were pinned to the board. Cork tiles glued on to cardboard could be used to create a similar display frame.

2 | Protecting displays

- Large sheets of card were decorated with food product packages. The items on display were covered with clear plastic so that they could be used again and again. They can also be stored easily without getting damaged.

3 | Creating interactive displays

- Below is an interactive display that can be modified and changed. The words are attached to the display with masking tape. The puppets can be removed so that the children can use them to create their story.

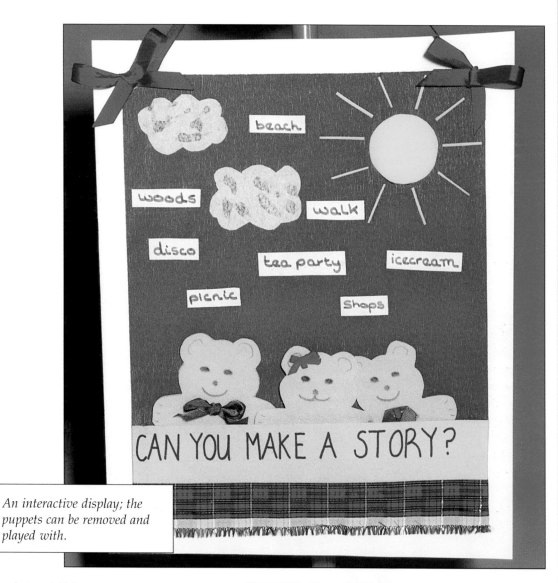

An interactive display; the puppets can be removed and played with.

Creating displays in groups

Various views, scenes, settings, locations and environments are regularly illustrated by children. However, by using a variety of different materials and techniques the children can develop new skills and knowledge, and throughout the process they will also be learning how to co-operate and collaborate with each other. When working together as a team, the children can also successfully create a number of different displays which would be difficult for them to create alone.

Large wall-mounted displays can be created quite simply by layering and sequencing the back drop and the foreground images. Combining different techniques and materials enables the children to arrange and rearrange their work, to portray the scene in perspective.

1 The sheep pig

■ This display, inspired by the Dick King-Smith novel was created on a hessian background. The sheep were made from a card template and were covered with rectangles of knitting. The hills, trees, fence, pig and the farmer were made from felt shapes and attached using fabric glue.

A scene created by a group of children.

A display arranged by the children utilising fabric, cardboard and templates.

2 In the street

■ This simple display was made from knitted rectangles and organised by a group of children. The houses were mounted on to a hessian background with fabric glue. Those shown at the front of the scene are larger than those at the rear.

A three-dimensional scene created by the children.

3 | A three-dimensional scene

■ 'The fish who could wish' shows how to create a three-dimensional scene using different types of paper, such as sugar-paper, card and tissue-paper and simple folding and attachment techniques. Hooks were made by opening out one end of a paper clip and sticking it to the board with masking tape. Some of the fish were attached to these with nylon thread and are able to rotate. The layers of torn tissue were arranged on a display panel after the paper-clip hooks were attached.

A display showing layering of paper and paint, creating a three-dimensional effect.

4 | Ancient Greece

■ This view shows how random sky paintings were created and overlaid with foreground contours made from sugar paper. The buildings were made from small rectangles of card, which were decorated and folded before being arranged on the display.

49

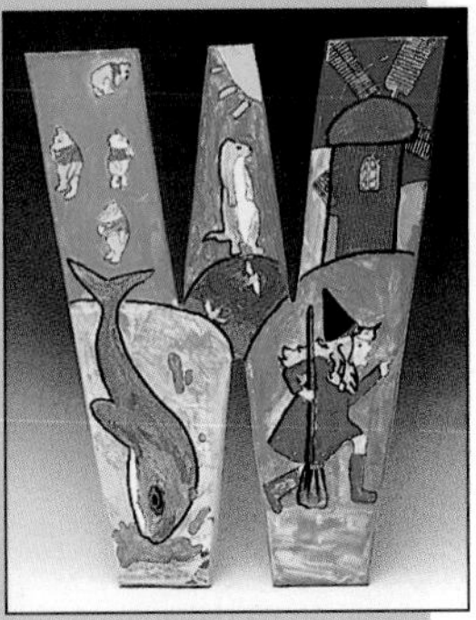

Windows

Using windows as areas for display

Windows can be decorated to brighten uninteresting internal areas and to help mask unattractive spaces outside the building. Sun-screen window decorations can be designed to be viewed both internally and externally, and can help deflect sunlight and generally improve the ambience of the room.

Some simple window displays will be enhanced if the external environment against which the display will be viewed – the backdrop of the display – is considered when the display area is being selected.

1 Floral windows

- Masking an unattractive external space and creating a semi-permanent internal display area can be achieved by:
  - creating a paper pattern of the window area
  - measuring, marking and cutting out paper templates
  - using the templates on cellophane or other similar material
  - temporarily joining the final shape designs together
  - using clear glue on areas where overlap is required
  - permanently taping the shapes together using black or coloured tape
  - firmly attaching the display to the window with tape or glue.

This area has been transformed by the stained glass effect on the windows.

An attractive alternative to conventional curtains

2 Fabric sun-screens

- This sun-screen was created from a single sheet of decorated cotton material folded at the top and simply stitched, to form a pelmet. The random images on the fabric were created with fabric paint and crayons, and the flower pots were painted using a stencil (page 63). A wooden rod attached to the wall by hooks holds the material in place.

Creative silhouettes create an effective display on a window.

3 Silhouettes

- The figures shown here are enhanced by the backdrop of trees. The figures and masks were made from black sugar paper and arranged on the window using double-sided tape. A template for a figure can be found on page 64.

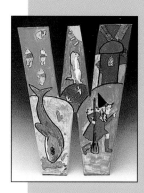

4 Card sun-screen decorations

- The sun-screen is bordered by coloured tape. Strips of folded card were stapled to the outside of the display area to form hangers. The hangers were disguised with sticky shapes – circles or triangles – and a garden cane was used to brace the sun-screen across the breadth of the window. It was attached to the window using existing window supports. Alternatively the canes can be hung over plastic cup-hooks or other similar attachment resources depending on the window frame material. The sun-screens can be used continually for display purposes as long as the images displayed are attached to the card with masking tape.

The sun-screen window decorations have been made by taping two pieces of coloured card together.

Display tip

Shape templates, mounted on to card, can be created by:
- cutting existing shapes and images from magazines and newspapers
- generating computer images or by using clip-art
- creating simple designs on grid paper such as squared or hexagonal paper
- folding card to create shapes with one or more axes of symmetry.

51

KEY IDEAS – *The A–Z of Display*

Free-standing and three-dimensional
mounted Christmas figures

Models on display are particularly useful; they can be arranged and rearranged by the children. Three-dimensional Christmas models can made from everyday household items. Some aspects of Christmas displays can be designed to be used from year to year; a nativity scene, for example, can be added to over the years, linking present and past pupils.

1 Free-standing figures in fabric

■ These figures were made from soft wadding covered with fine dish cloth material. String was tied tightly around pieces of material to create the heads. Cardboard tubes filled with plasticine, to create stability, were used for each body. The figures were arranged on a bed of shredded paper inside a cardboard box stable. Each year, the children cut, wrap and temporarily sew fabric around the figures to make changes to their appearance.

These figures were created to be dressed by the children from year to year.

2 Free-standing figures made from bottles

■ Empty plastic bottles filled with sand for stability form the body of these figures. Wadding was placed beneath the fabric to form the heads of the characters. Wool and string were used to secure the fabric in place. The display is arranged on a fabric-covered table top. A silhouette scene forms the background.

Christmas story figures made from empty plastic drinks bottles.

52

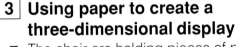

The choir are paintings of the children in the class.

3 Using paper to create a three-dimensional display

■ The choir are holding pieces of paper that were stapled to the wall to give a three-dimensional effect. The images were attached to the wall-board by stapling. The foil lettering was made from letter stencils.

4 Using a cardboard box to create a three-dimensional display

■ Santa is made from a child's red jumper that was modified by attaching card buttons. He was stuffed with newspaper so that he is light and will sit in the decorated cardboard box chimney, stapled to the wall-board. His head is a circle of card with a tissue paper hat attachment. The net was used to support the display and also give the impression of clouds. Stars made from foil can also be attached.

Using a cardboard box to create 'When Santa got stuck up the chimney'.

53

Yum-yum

Food as a stimulus for display

A number of techniques can be incorporated into any project, topic or theme. 'Yum-yum' is a food-based example of how to cut, shape and join a variety of different materials creatively. Techniques include the use of card and papier mâché and using reclaimed materials.

1 Using papier mâché

■ The cans are made from strips of card bent over a rectangle of card that is covered with screwed-up newspaper to give depth. The strips are held in place with layers of masking tape and then covered with papier mâché. The shapes were painted with the designs using paint mixed with PVA to make it glossy. They were attached to the cardboard background with glue.

This three-dimensional 'drinks' display is made from cardboard covered with papier mâché.

This display of publicity posters shows how a theme can be used in close observation work.

2 Close observation

■ An interesting display of publicity posters was designed after the children carefully examined drinks containers. They were made by using felt-tipped pens on card.

54

An interesting publicity montage using reclaimed materials.

3 Using reclaimed materials

■ Empty sweet wrappers were attached to the lid of a cardboard box to create a free-standing display advertising the products available in the school shop.

An enlargement of an original sweet tube.

4 Enlarging an ordinary object to create a display

■ An original cardboard confectionery tube was reproduced and enlarged to create this effective free-standing display. It was covered with screwed-up tissue-paper shapes to create a three-dimensional effect.

55

zany

Imaginative 'zany' displays

designed to attract attention

Vivid displays can be created by bringing the work of individual children together. Simple activities can be organised in the classroom or the school generally. The children should choose their own designs, but their work must be bright, colourful and, where possible, humorous.

1 Crazy mugs
- The mugs were displayed on boxes covered by an attractive fabric hanger that complements the colours used in the mugs. Detailed drawings of the mugs were attached to the wall-board behind the arrangement.

The elaborate designs on the mugs were made by individual children.

2 Lively letters
- Each letter was designed to be of a similar size in order to create an alphabet frieze.

Each letter of the alphabet has been attractively decorated using pens and pencils.

56

These attractive suns were made from a variety of materials.

3 Zany suns

■ Bright and vibrant colours were selected to create these lively suns. Shiny thread was also used to attach the suns to the cotton fabric which was stapled to the wall-board.

4 A zany arrangement

■ These jazzy clowns were made by cutting, shaping and joining paper to create individual characteristics on each. They were arranged on a bright textured background in a haphazard fashion to reflect the clowns themselves.

These colourful paper clowns create a bright and attractive display.

57

KEY IDEAS – The A–Z of Display

Templates to photocopy and cut out.
They can be used to create the
displays on pages 8, 11, 14 and 20.

Decorative frames that can be
photocopied and coloured in by
the children. Further ideas for
frames are on pages 16–17.

59

A template to photocopy and attach to card to make small versions of the vases on page 26. Alternatively, photocopy and enlarge the template, transfer each section (apart from the flaps) separately on to strong card and assemble with masking tape.

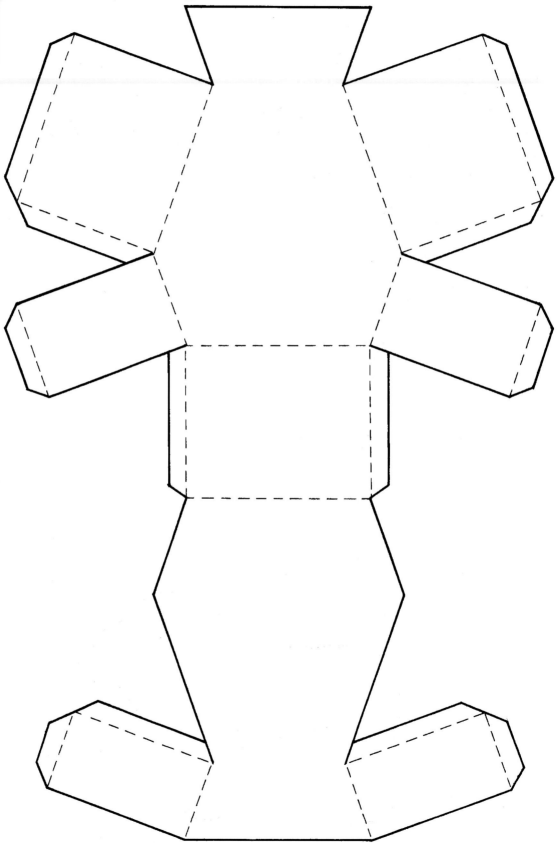

KEY IDEAS – *The A–Z of Display*

© Folens (copiable page)

Animal templates to photocopy
and transfer on to balsa wood to
create the mobile on page 30.

Templates that can be used to create the number board on page 39.

KEY IDEAS – *The A–Z of Display*

© Folens (copiable page)

Paper faces to photocopy and cut out. Mount on to a black background, as on page 36.

A flower-pot stencil to create part of the fabric sun-screen on page 50. Photocopy and transfer it on to card and cut out the holes using a craft knife.

63

Photocopy and enlarge this figure and transfer it on to black paper to create the window silhouettes on page 51.